TERRY DISCHINGER
MITCH RICHMOND
WES UNSELD
BERNARD KING
TOM GUGLIOTTA
EARL MONROE
JUWAN HOWARD
WALT BELLAMY
ELVIN HAYES
CHRIS WEBBER
JEFF RULAND
JAHIDI WHITE

THE HISTORY OF THE WASHINGTON WIZARDS

CREATIVE EDUCATION
AARON FRISCH

Published by Creative Education, 123 South Broad Street, Mankato, MN 56001

Creative Education is an imprint of The Creative Company.

Designed by Rita Marshall

Photos by Active Images, Allsport, AP/Wide World, Rich Kane, NBA Photos, SportsChrome

Copyright © 2002 Creative Education. International copyright reserved in all countries.

No part of this book may be reproduced in any form

without written permission from the publisher.

Library of Congress Cataloging-in-Publication Data

Frisch, Aaron. The history of the Washington Wizards / by Aaron Frisch.

p. cm. – (Pro basketball today)   ISBN 1-58341-118-6

1. Washington Wizards (Basketball team)—History—

Juvenile literature. [1. Washington Wizards (Basketball team)—History.

2. Basketball—History.] I. Title. II. Series.

GV885.52.W37 F75 2001   796.323′64′09753—dc21   00-047335

First Edition 9 8 7 6 5 4 3 2 1

WASHINGTON, D.C., THE CAPITAL OF THE UNITED STATES, IS THE ONLY AMERICAN CITY THAT IS NOT PART OF ONE OF THE 50

states. Washington occupies a section of government-owned land called the District of Columbia (D.C. for short) located between Maryland and Virginia. The city was named after America's first president, George Washington, who personally selected the site on which to build the town.

Many tourists travel to Washington to visit such famous buildings as the Capitol and White House and such renowned landmarks as the Washington Monument and Lincoln Memorial. Yet Washington is rich in more than just government history; it also has a long and storied

WALT BELLAMY

sports tradition. One of those traditions involves a National Basketball Association (NBA) franchise named the Wizards, which settled in the nation's capital in 1972.

*The only NBA player to outscore Walt Bellamy in **1961–62** was legendary center Wilt Chamberlain.*

{FROM THE PACKERS TO "THE PEARL"} The Wizards franchise started out in Chicago, Illinois, in 1961 as a team called the Packers. Although the team went only 18–62 its first season, it featured a young star named Walt Bellamy. The first-year center led Chicago by scoring 31 points and grabbing 19 rebounds per game, earning NBA Rookie of the Year honors.

After the season, the team changed its name to the Zephyrs and added sharpshooting rookie forward Terry Dischinger. Still, the team struggled, and the city of Chicago seemed disinterested in the franchise. So, in 1963, the team's owners moved the franchise to Baltimore, Maryland, and renamed it the Bullets.

CHRIS WEBBER

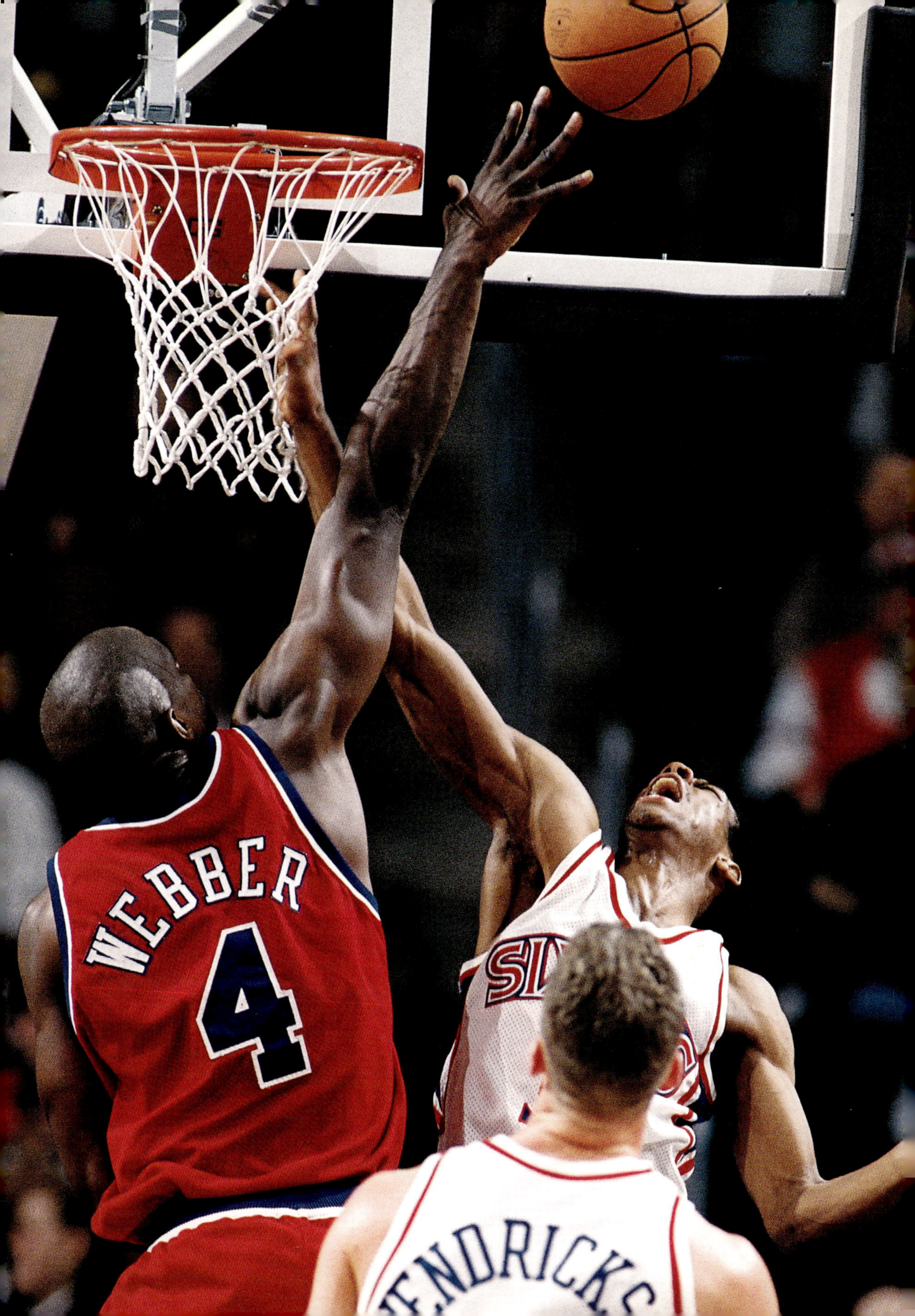

WEBBER
4
ENDRICKS

Earl Monroe led the Bullets in scoring in his first four NBA seasons.

EARL MONROE

In Baltimore, the Bullets showed improvement behind the efforts of Bellamy, forward Bailey Howell, and guards Don Ohl and Kevin Loughery. In 1964–65, the team posted a 37–43 record and surprised the league by driving as far as the Western Division Finals in the playoffs. Two years later, however, the Bullets struggled again, limping to a 20–61 record.

In 1967, Baltimore brought in a new coach and a new star. The coach was Gene Shue, and the star was a 6-foot-3 guard named Earl "the Pearl" Monroe, taken with the second pick in the 1967 NBA Draft. Monroe had averaged more than 40 points per game in his final college season. Still, some NBA scouts viewed his game as more style than substance.

In his rookie season, Monroe put all such doubts to rest and won over Baltimore fans by scoring 24 points per game. His array of dazzling

> Don Ohl was one of eight Bullets players to average at least 10 points a game in **1965–66**.

DON OHL

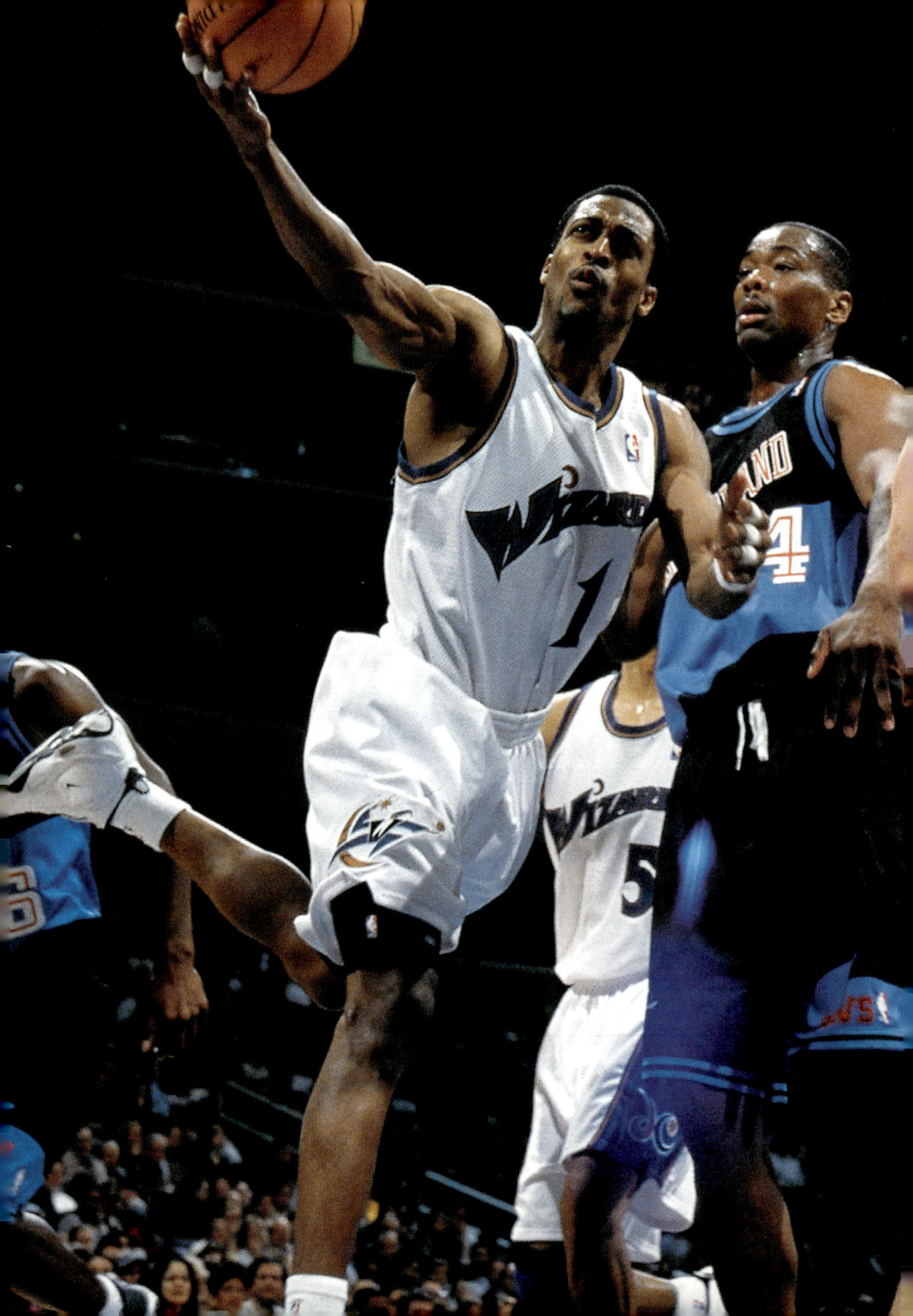

Like Earl Monroe, Rod Strickland was equally adept at scoring and passing.

ROD STRICKLAND

moves and ability to make seemingly impossible shots left opponents shaking their heads. "That Monroe is unbelievable," said New York Knicks guard Walt Frazier after trying to stop the Bullets' young star. "I don't think the Pearl saw the basket on some of those shots, but he's that kind of shooter."

{WINNING WITH WES} Monroe, Loughery, and forward Jack Marin gave Baltimore a strong scoring attack, but the team lacked a powerful post player and was often badly beaten on the boards. In the 1968 NBA Draft, the Bullets cured that problem by using their top pick on muscular 6-foot-7 center Wes Unseld from the University of Louisville.

Unseld was the shortest center in the NBA, but he made up for it with his incredible strength. As opponents quickly learned, once he got into rebounding position, he was virtually impossible to move. In

> The explosive Bullets offense scored 100 or more points in 36 straight games in **1968–69**.

WES UNSELD

1968–69, Unseld grabbed 18 boards and scored nearly 14 points per game—performances that earned him the NBA Most Valuable Player award as just a rookie.

"Wes is just beautiful," said Bullets forward Ray Scott. "The other team shoots, Wes goes for the ball, and the rest of us go charging downcourt. He hits one of our guards at midcourt with one of those two-handed, over-the-head passes of his, and somebody else winds up with an easy layup."

In **1970–71**, forward Jack Marin led the Bullets to a 52-point victory over Portland.

With the stout center and Monroe leading the way, the Bullets surged to an NBA-best 57–25 record in 1968–69. Two years later, Baltimore capped a 42–40 season by battling all the way to the NBA Finals. There, the Milwaukee Bucks and star center Lew Alcindor stunned the Bullets by winning the series in a four-game sweep. Still, with the Bullets riding Unseld's powerful shoulders, Baltimore fans were confident that a title would soon be theirs.

{THE BULLETS HIT THE MARK} The Bullets underwent a series of major changes over the next few years. Having made Unseld their centerpiece, the Bullets traded Monroe to New York in 1971. A year later, they traded with Houston for forward Elvin Hayes. Then,

MITCH KUPCHAK

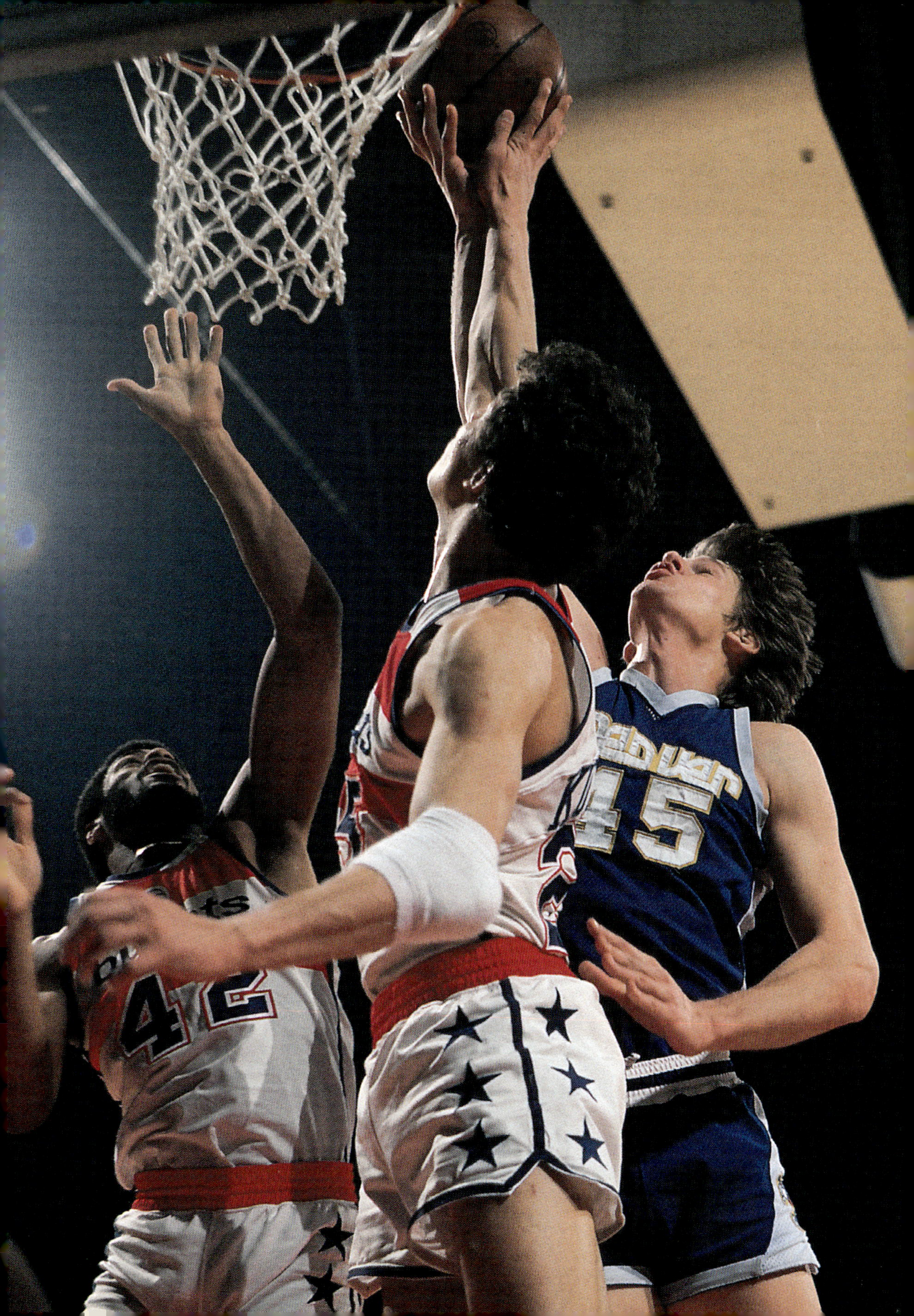
45
42

after the 1972–73 season, the team moved into a new arena on the out-

skirts of nearby Washington.

The Bullets were an instant hit with Washington fans. A big reason

for their popularity was Hayes. Known as the "Big E," the forward aver-

aged at least 20 points and 11 rebounds year after year. "The Big E has

been a gem since the day he arrived," said Coach Shue. "He has worked very hard. I couldn't be more pleased."

Over the next three seasons, Hayes helped Washington post winning records each year with the support of such players as guards Phil Chenier and Mike Riordan. He also helped lead the Bullets back to the NBA Finals in 1975. Unfortunately, they again fell short of a championship, this time losing to the Golden State Warriors in one of the most stunning upsets in league history.

Forward Elvin Hayes represented the Bullets in eight straight All-Star Games.

In 1976, the Bullets hired Dick Motta as their new head coach. A year later, they added Bob Dandridge, a quick forward who could score in bunches. With Dandridge lined up alongside Hayes and Unseld, Washington had perhaps the best frontcourt in the NBA. Other solid players included reserve forward Mitch Kupchak and guards Kevin Grevey and Tom Henderson.

ELVIN HAYES

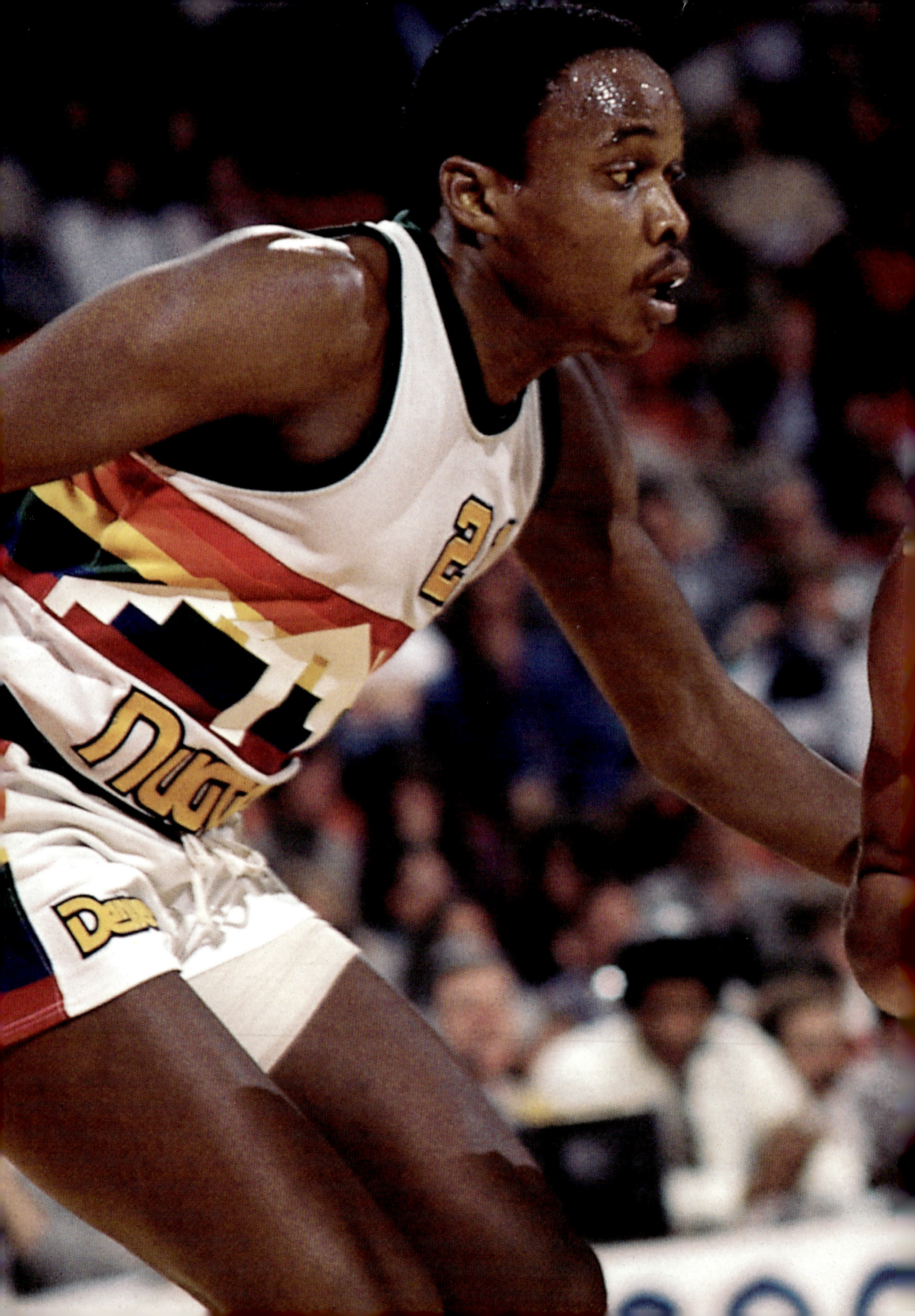

Steady guard Jeff Malone averaged more than 20 points a game in seven seasons.

This lineup went a mere 44–38 in 1977–78. But the Bullets hit their stride in the playoffs, toppling the Atlanta Hawks, San Antonio Spurs, and Philadelphia 76ers to reach the NBA Finals for the third time in franchise history. Their opponent this time was the Seattle SuperSonics, who had come out of nowhere to reach the Finals.

After six games, the series stood tied. In the deciding seventh game in front of a raucous Seattle crowd, the SuperSonics tried to erase a slim Bullets' lead late in the fourth quarter. But Washington was not about to let another championship slip away. Unseld grabbed two critical rebounds in the final minute to preserve a 105–99 victory and give the Bullets their first NBA title.

The Bullets nearly repeated as champs the next season. After posting an NBA-best 54–28 record, they charged back to the Finals, where

Forward Bob Dandridge led the team in steals as the Bullets rolled to the **1978** NBA championship.

BOB DANDRIDGE

they again faced the SuperSonics. Washington emerged victorious in game one, but Seattle exacted revenge by sweeping the next four games and claiming the title.

{RELOADING IN THE '80s} As it turned out, that was the mighty Bullets' last run. In 1980, Coach Motta left town, and a year later, Unseld retired and Hayes was traded to Houston. New coach Gene

Shue, back for a second stint with the team, rebuilt his lineup around rugged center Jeff Ruland and forward Rick Mahorn—a pair known as the "Bruise Brothers"—but the Bullets fell into a slump.

Washington brought in several new players over the next few years in an attempt to find a winning combination again. Among these players were forward Cliff Robinson, high-scoring guards Gus Williams and Jeff Malone, and 7-foot-7 center Manute Bol. In 1985–86, Malone scored 22 points per game, and Bol led the league in blocked shots. Still, the team posted another losing record, and Shue was fired late in the season.

In 1986, the Bullets added center Moses Malone, who had led the Philadelphia 76ers to an NBA championship just three years earlier. Still, the team struggled. In 1988, the Bullets hired former center and local hero Wes Unseld as their new head coach. Unseld knew he had his

Center Manute Bol tied an NBA record with 11 blocks in one half of a **1985–86** game.

MANUTE BOL

Center Jeff Ruland led Washington in rebounding for five straight seasons in the early **'80s**.

JEFF RULAND

24

work cut out for him, especially since Moses Malone had left for Atlanta after just two seasons in a Bullets uniform.

Fortunately, the Bullets had a player ready to pick up the slack. That player was forward Bernard King, who had been one of the NBA's top scorers with the New York Knicks in the early 1980s before a devastating knee injury in 1985 nearly ended his career. After the injury, many fans wondered if he would ever play again, let alone dominate as he once had. But the veteran refused to give up.

In 1988–89 and 1989–90, King went over and around defenders to score more than 20 points per game. And in 1990–91, he capped his miraculous comeback by netting 28 points per game and once again earning a place on the All-Star team. "To come back after the entire knee was reconstructed . . . [is] one of the most special feelings in the

> In a **1990–91** game, Bernard King scored 52 of his team's franchise-record 161 points.

BERNARD KING

world," King said. "And it's something that I'm awfully proud of."

{A CAPITAL REVIVAL} King gave Washington some great performances, as did such teammates as guard Darrell Walker and forward Harvey Grant. But after the Bullets posted a mere 30–52 record in 1990–91, the team continued to reshape its lineup. Among the additions were centers Pervis Ellison and 7-foot-7 Gheorghe Muresan, guard

Michael Adams, and forwards Tom Gugliotta and Calbert Cheaney. The team had talent, but it seemed to lack leadership on the court. As a result, Washington suffered several losing seasons.

In 1994, Jim Lynam replaced Unseld as head coach. A bigger story that year, however, was the Bullets' new young forward duo of Juwan Howard and Chris Webber. Howard arrived first via the 1994 NBA Draft and immediately became the team's leading scorer and rebounder. Then, early in the 1994–95 season, Washington added Webber by trading Gugliotta and future draft picks to Golden State.

Howard and Webber had been college teammates at the University of Michigan, and their reunion in Washington gave Bullets fans hope. With the two young forwards and Muresan forming a formidable frontcourt, the Bullets finally rose in the standings. In 1995–96, they jumped

Forward Juwan Howard provided much of the Bullets' firepower in the late **1990s**.

JUWAN HOWARD

to a respectable 39–43 record—an improvement of 18 victories over the previous season.

> Center Gheorghe Muresan shot an NBA-high 60 percent from the floor in **1996–97**.

To get a player who could distribute the ball to their young stars, the Bullets then traded for point guard Rod Strickland. Although Strickland had earned a reputation for his sometimes disruptive behavior, he was also one of the NBA's top assists men. "[We] have a lot of young, athletic, talented big people," said Coach Lynam, "and to plant an experienced guard like Rod with them, I think that is a huge plus."

This talented lineup continued moving up in 1996–97, leading Washington to the playoffs for the first time in 10 years. Webber and Howard combined for nearly 40 points and 18 rebounds per game, Strickland paced the team's offense, and Cheaney and forward Tracy Murray added great perimeter shooting.

GHEORGHE MURESAN

{WEBBER OUT, WIZARDS IN} Following that season, the Bullets changed their name to the Wizards and moved into the brand-new MCI Center. Under new coach Bernie Bickerstaff, Washington went 42–40 the next season—a disappointing record for a team with so much talent. The young Wizards were painfully inconsistent, often beating contenders one night and losing to the league's bottom feeders the next.

In **1999–00**, long-range bomber Tracy Murray knocked down 113 three-point shots.

So, in a bold move, the Wizards traded Webber in the off-season for veteran guard Mitch Richmond. Even though Richmond was on the downside of his brilliant career, he was still a potent scorer, and Washington hoped he would give the team more balance and maturity. Richmond played well, but the Wizards faded to 18–32 in 1998–99.

Early in 2000, a new star came to town: former NBA guard

TRACY MURRAY

At 290 pounds, Jahidi White outmuscled opponents as he worked the boards.

JAHIDI WHITE

Quickness and a deft shooting touch made guard Richard Hamilton a rising star.

RICHARD HAMILTON

Michael Jordan, who joined the Wizards as part owner and president of basketball operations. As a player, Jordan had led the Chicago Bulls to

> Washington fans hoped that swingman Tyrone Nesby would help turn the Wizards' fortunes around.

six NBA titles, and he was determined to continue adding players like powerful young center Jahidi White to make Washington a champion as well. "I'm going to have my imprint and fingerprints all over this organization," he promised. "I look forward to turning it around."

Since its inception in 1961, the Wizards franchise has played under four different names in three different cities. But throughout those changes, the organization's commitment to winning has never faltered, resulting in one NBA championship and several other close calls. Today's Wizards hope that this commitment will soon make Washington the capital of the basketball world once again.

TYRONE NESBY

WITHDRAWN